Poetic Reveries

Seema Sharma

First Published in 2021

Becomeshakespeare.com
One Point Six Technologies Pvt Ltd.
119-123, 1st Floor, Building J2,
B - Wing, WadalaTruck Terminal,
Wadala East, Mumbai,
Maharashtra, India, 400022.
T:+91 8080226699

ISBN - 978-93-5438-399-1

Contents

Contents

Contents

Contents

Contents

Rhythm of Rain

Shimmering drops fall from heaven above
Oh, this downpour brings cheer to my parched soul
Pretty pearly droplets sprawling on my hand
That touch so soothing like a bewitching-rand

Gentle breeze blowing with the rain along
The rhythm of falling drops feel like a song
The dripping trees merrily sing their own tune
Makes me elated, as if listened to a bassoon

Dancing leaves look so exhilarated
When drizzle drops fall upon made em wet
Lush greenery, laughing flowers..oh, so awesome
Scented blossoms look so sweet when they bloom

Behold, the watering clouds look so obese
As though they are ailing from some disease
Releasing water afterward they look relaxed though
Rain has taken birth from the womb of Earth below

Oh, this petrichor has an embalming effect
Scented sand smells....O, just perfect!
Showering from the blue looks so glorious
Pleases my soul, everything becomes auspicious

It's like blessings from the blue
This rainbow afterwards spreading its wondrous hue
The surrounding becomes so enriched with enhanced beauty
Heavenly drops pouring down makes this Earth feel glee

Seema ✍

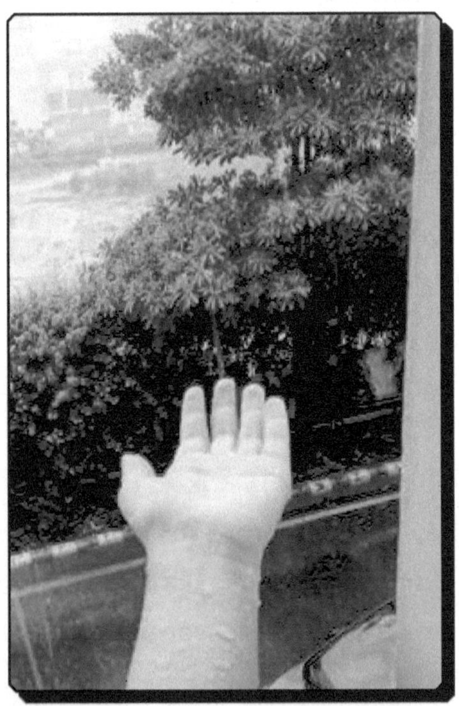

She Walks in Rain

He was like a summer rain

And she, a parched

land

He poured himself down

Drenched her all around

Made her look embellished

With all kinda lovely blossoms

She was adorned and burgeoned

Monsoon of her life began

Sprinkles of droplets pouring

She had awaited in all her life span

She, no more bleak but fully ornate

Rejoiced and emblazoned with each touch of drizzle- drops

It was Spring in her life

He stayed there for a while

Hues of myriad flowers on her bosom smiled

Shaped her in sweet form

Overjoyed she sparkled with sprinkling- shower

for quite long

But
It so happened..
He, with his droplets couldn't stay any longer
Moved on...
Yes, he moved away with the rushing winds
Leaving the rainbow as his left out sign

She, now again a withered land, still
Awaits for sweet shower
On her dreary and dried hand
Uplifting herself toward her Heavens
Hopes for the revival of rain
To bedeck herself once again

Seema ✍

Immortality

BEAUTIFUL THINGS remain forever.
Forever is our SACRED SOUL.
MEMORIES are dwelt in our heart, they do perish never.
Never do the KIND SOULS die, they are eternal ever.

LOVELY MUSIC soothes our soul.
Provides solace, peace and so much pleasure.
Oh, that sublime tunes, merry songs!
Pours the melodies out in our ears.

NATURE'S BOUNTIES are at it's best.
Those hills, mountains, rills and ridges;
Oh, capture our heart n eyes, give so much delight!
Remains stored in our soul like a divine- light.

SOOTHING- SOFT WORDS spoken with mirth,
Permanently they stay in our heart.
Oh, immeasurable Joy that they do provide!
All listeners go dumbstruck.

Immortal is our SOUL.
Immortal is all what BEAUTY contains.

Immortal are the FEELINGS.
Immortal is a singer's SOULFUL RENDITION.
Immortal are the DEEDS committed with sincerity
Immortal is TRUTH, and so is BEAUTY.

Thus, let's applause the things
That brings cheers to us!
Let's be soft and Noble in our words.
Let's be soulful and do the things out with truth and passion!
 Since immortality lies in virtues, not in vices!

Seema✍

I Have Realized..

I have realized what Life means
Life does not mean existing
Life means living fruitfully
Living constructively, living joyfully

I have realized what Love means
Love does not mean what you want is important
Love means the other person's needs are paramount
Love implies giving unconditionally ,Uncomplainingly

I have realized what Beauty means
Beauty does not mean something that appeals to the eyes
Beauty means that appeals to the soul
Beauty comes from inside, having a kind and gentle heart

I have realized what Hate means
Hate does not mean detesting the person
Hate means disliking the vices they possess
Hate means unliking someone's manner of some wrong
doings when they do

I have realized what Mistake means

Mistake does not mean not doing incorrect things

Mistake means committing some follies deliberately, doing something wrong intentionally

I have realized what Maturity means

Maturity does not mean attaining adulthood

Maturity means considering others opinions and never disrespecting them

Maturity implies acting with wisdom

I have realized what Smile means

A smiling face does not mean one is happy

Smiling person means he knows how to be joyful by his pleasing disposition

The person with a smile wants to win other's love

I have realized so many things in life

I am living my life, I have attained love

I smile usually, I commit mistakes

I behave with maturity, I hate none

Though I have realized all these things

But I fail to understand why People don't realize!

Why people don't take things positively

Why do people despise each other

I fail to understand why
I fail to understand why

Seema ✍

Traces of Innocence

Childhood is the stage, so so pure
It's the best phase for a being, for sure
No strife, conflict, clash or any friction
Pure joys and mirth without any affliction

Innocence is the second name for it; so divine
It's the Springtime to be enjoyed; so sublime
Greenness and merriment prevail in this tender age
Ethereal it is of course with so much craze

How beautiful the tiny- tots look when they are at play
Their faces shine bright with blithe throughout the day
Sans shrewdness, sans vile, sans malice
Charming and sweet smile they wear on their angelic faces

Swinging on the trees, running merrily
Leaping like frogs, singing joyfully
Running around the squirrels, chasing butterflies, skipping
ropes.. so much for enjoying

O, what a blissful and celestial fun!

I wish the childhood remains for years to come!

No worries, pains or any fret or whine,

How wonderful the world is with lovely kids in their prime!

Seema ✍

Nature's Bounties

The cascading streams and the water- flowing
Say us never to stop, keep going

Never be the one who grudges all day long
Hurdles-hindrances come and will come
Try to sing a happy song

These blossoms make us laugh
It's not that they never face the windy-storm!
But they have learnt to face every odds for long

Keep sparkling though the skies are grey sometimes
Beams of the Sun
have this to say
in its mute but shining tone

Keep your goals as high as the mountain top
keep doing all efforts but never you stop

The vast sky, far and blue

Say us to dream high and never bid adieu

Look at that lustre, that sheen the sunbeams spread!

Be merry all the time and keep moving ahead

Rejoice, regale and never wither or whine

 Whispers the blowing breeze gently in the ears of mine

Seema✍

Optimism

When Hope starts dwindling;
When darkness prevails around;
When this world casts a dreary sound...

O thou!
Listen the song your soul is serenading;
This is an echo that signals the dawn is approaching.

Fear not, grow flowers..they will surely bloom.
For Autumn has gone, here comes the spring.
Look at the swallow perching and fluttering its wing.
Rainbow with its vibrant hues.. spreading delight.
Keep sparkling, don't lessen your light.

O thou!
Catch up every drop the heaven dost fall.
It's an elixir..an ocean divine..
Life's not a bed of roses you know.
Thorns and prickles make us strong though.

It's the inner strength that counts.

Go on to meet your destination.

Do not be carried away by the temptation.

O, Thou!

Look at the stars that always shine.

Never you go fade, fret or whine!

Smile more for the dawn has arrived :)

Hope.. hope and sing like a bird,

For the Hope is a bird that perches in the soul.

Seema✍

Revival of the Heart

Let's sow the seeds of love to nourish the withered feelings'.

Let's bring that Spark that had been there but seems to be lost now and demands healing.

Let's bridge the gap that seems to be widened up with that span of time.

Let's embark on the moon and enjoy the beauty of the sublime.

Let's talk about you and me and withdraw ourselves from this mundane world.

Let's enrich the greenery that surrounded us once... now looks pale and dull.

Let's renew our bond and cherish the dreams me and you weaved together.

Let's tie up the love vibes' with our souls that could connect us together forever.

Let's meet in the cherished dreams and refresh the immortal souls.

Let's make love that remains forever in years to come.

Let's be one and never part from each other.

Let's do...let's do..

Seema✍

I Wish..!!!

I wish I were a bird!

I would have taken thee to the land..

Where there are only Joys with.. Fragrant- flowers, blooming-blossoms and Sunbeams.

I wish I were a star!

I would have shone bright like you sparkle;

Would have accompanied you till the dawn appears,

Thy sparkling Rays would have mingled with mine.

I wish I were a bird!

I would have flown directly to your embrace,

Would have crossed miles without any fear though;

Heaven would be so near as bliss!

I wish I were a lyre!

I would have sounded melodious when thy fingers pressed upon me to play,

Thy touch would have soothed my soul;

When the strings of it would have binded me like thy heart's crossbow.

I wish I were a song!

When you would have serenaded me from your lips;

Would have moved thousands to enchant;

I would have relished each lyric when you have sung!

I wish I were with you!

We would have dreamt together..shone like stars,

Flown like a winged bird', played soothing tunes, chanted delightful songs,

Would have lived together forever happily.

I wish...I just wish!!!!

Seema✍

Recollections

Capturing the moments in the camera of my heart,
I take joy in retrospection of my sweet past.

Those were the days...we used to share every little thing with elation.
All the memorabilias still come alive to me in quick succession.

We called those feelings, "Beautiful; sacred, they would never perish,
The moments, in the coming time, we will always cherish".

Such precious and indelible are the memories; so divine.
Never would they leave my heart, soul and mind.

They are merely the memories now, that would never ever go.
In my dreams they visit every now and then, you know!

But, why so?? ... .

It seems those tender feelings in thee, are on the wane.

No more pleasure, thou seem to get, rather have shown some disdain.

Did the Time slay thy all emotions?

Have you forgotten them altogether, no passions?

I wonder.. !

Time was never so tall that stood between our love, so pure!

Or else thy love has vanished into thin air, for sure!

Seema ✍

Nature Tells Me About You

This Blowing Breeze seems to say about you
It signifies you would be walking along the woods you wish
to

These Swinging Swallows are a signal of your being joyous
You would be making merriment with your own choice

Sparkling Sunshine tells me how you make others glad
You would be laughing out loudly with the humorous jokes
you crack

This Elegant Evening indicates how you would have attired
yourself
You would indeed be in your favourite eve dress

Blooming Blossoms with butterflies tell me about the way
you smile
You would be smiling with the people you admire

Dew Drops on the green grass conveys something to me
You would be sitting in the lap of nature with much glee

Setting Sun with it's serenity speaks about your being in isolation
You would be having your quiet time in God's adulation

Now, you are not here with me though
Nature tells me everything about you!
Waiting for the day when you'll be here
Together we will make our life worthwhile, dear!

Seema ✍

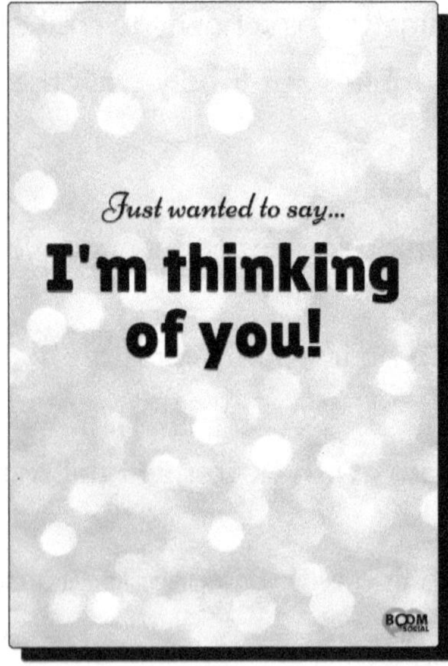

Words that Resonate

The words we utter, reverberate all around
They are the reflection of our true self, they resound

Words are the source to reach masses
Words are the means to remove their clashes

Words we speak gently convey our elegance
People get drawn when we speak with eloquence

Words reflect our inner spirit well
How much compassion and love we possess, they tell

Words are neither the toys' nor the fragile hearts' to be broken
Nor are they the trust' to be shaken

Words can cement the bonds and expand mutual ties
They work as the keys to unlock agonised hearts' and erase their mute cries

Words spoken with sweetness, bring smiles
Words, when spoken harshly, make people go far away miles

The soft words we articulate, resonate like musical beats
Their echo reaches the soul which our heart feeds

Thus, let's speak sweet and lovely words
Speak the words that never hurt others.

Let's use them carefully, meticulously!
Let's speak veraciously and prudently!

Seema ✍

This Time Too Shall Pass

Though the weather is stormy and dark
We all seem tired and have lost much spark

It's true we are sailing in the ocean of sorrow
Night is stormy but it will not last though

There will be a dawn of new hopes
Better things will fall into place

Time will change the things altogether
It will bring more peace and good weather

If winter comes, can Spring be far behind?
Let's think positive and scare away the wind

Do not despair but Kindle a light
Weave your dreams and look at the bright sight

Miseries are soon to be vanished
Joys and happiness are to be replaced with

We are all together we are gonna alright
Let's face the odds with all our might

This time too shall pass
This time too shall pass

Seema ✍

A Void...

There is stillness and silence allwhere
Happiness seem to get sunk in deep slumber
An air of greyness looms large
Life is nothing more than a mirage

Oh, an eerie feeling has creeped in
No charm and enthusiasm within
A void is cropped up inside of me
Everything looks so dull and boring

Laughter like Sunshine has become faint
Life is now meaningless and quaint
The brightness also looks pale
No delights, joys or elation to hail

It has happened since you have gone
Gone is the sweetness in every song and tune
Your absence has caused melancholia
Alienation from you has built in me kinda phobia

All rays of hope and expectancy have dimmed
No prospect or possibility seems to usher in
I have been left with nothing but your memories alone
Still hoping against hope for your arrival back at my home

Ohh, I recall the time of togetherness
When we used to make merriment and were so blessed
All those moments.. they were not less than events
When everyday was Spring and there grew beautiful blossoms

Who can forget those days "divine"
Life was so joyous and truly "sublime"
Now you have walked away
Leaving the poignant feelings at bay

"Oh, Almighty God, do this favour ", I pray.
I fold up my hands in reverence of God, I say
May be He shower his precious Grace
Send you here to me and give me an embrace!

Seema ✑

Wielding My Pen

Chunks by chunks, probing for the words
From my mind, from my heart too
The words are strewn inside me
I wanna give them a shape
To transfigure them into a poem
To give them a soul
To create a piece worth reading for
I wanna write something insightful
Something that delights my senses
Something that pleases my critics too
A piece of wonder, some sort of creation
I wanna give birth to a masterpiece

I have wielded my pen to assist me
My all devotion goes to my writing
I will give life to a beautiful creativity
I find joy in writing
For it is my passion
It transports me to another world
In a world of intellectuals, the learned ones

A land of scholars, erudite people
A perfect place for honing my skills
I find myself amongst the lettered people
Oh, It feels so great!

Today I would write something worthwhile
I am overflowing with the words
Emotions start griping in..
A new dimension has taken form
A figurative status occuring inside
I wanna take that out and pen it down
To show it to the world
I want lovely people to read my stuff
I have reached to the level of bliss and exuberance
The way to go inside the reader's mind seems to be opened

Here I have given shape to a poem
But with no verse, meter or rhyme..

Philomath ✍

The Glorious Sun

O distant Shining Star, thou sparkle amidst the blue
Shimmering rays of thine spread all over with different hue

Thy beams enhance the beauty of the green
Penetrating from the delicate leaves, oh..it looks so serene

Behold! the lush green cluster of trees as though participating in some fashion show
Winning applause from all, standing tall in a row!

Thou art the reason to lay the beauty of a garden in such a splendid way
When thou radiate, all the things go sway

Thou always shine all over the planet without any prejudice
Be it North, East West or South.. you are suffice

Thou art the kindling hope that is provided to all with so much warmth
Thy shine falling on earth seem to cast a fluorescent charm

Thou keep the beings animated, be it humans or any figure
Thy light make them revital their spirit with much vigour

Thy beams on flowing water,make it dance, gleaming with lustre
That lovely moment look just perfect and unmatchable

I really wonder to see thy glorious side!
How majestically and magnificently thou spread world wide!

Seema ✍

Love

The love that binds the souls is divine
True love acts as a song in a rhyme
Keep singing, it will keep you joyous
Close your eyes and feel.. It's pious

Love is a melody
Keep playing it and feel glee
The tune of love you play is euphonious
It appeals to the ears, it's mellifluous

Love is a luscious food for the soul
It keeps you full and you want it more and more
It is the need for every being
It keeps you content and serene

Love is the finest balm
It heals the aching wounds and make you internally calm
The soothing effect it creates
You feel quite at ease

Love is a rainbow
It adds hues of joys and deletes sorrow
The incandescent colour it scatters
It makes the life luminous and better

Love is a kindling light
It radiates and makes your life bright
The darkness is removed as a whole
Love is very kind; you should love to the core

Love is a beautiful rose
It's fragrant petals embalms your nose
Keeps one mesmerised and savored
It's beauty is unsurpassed, grows in the garden of fortunate
lovers!

The feeling in love, is heavenly
It transports us in another world..really!
So, love and be loved without being weary
This is the message I wanna convey to all and sundry

Seema ✍

All pervasive: Who?

Who's that being, unknown?

Whose presence is felt, but not shown?

Who's hidden here within, like a soul?

Whose force carries us forward?

Who's channelising us ahead?

Who keeps the fear of the mind' at bay?

Who saves us from going astray?

Who keeps our uncontrollable blues' away?

Who uplifts us when we are at the doldrums?

Who makes us believe in our soul when we lose faith in ourselves?

Who keeps our safety assured?

Who sets the sail when we're overpowered by a storm?

Who is this imperceptible, invisible form?

That one and only one is-

The Supreme Power

A Divinity, an Almighty God

He is though ethereal

But exists in real

He is though indiscernible
But pervades all over
He's Omnipresent
But without any colour, caste or age
He's though ubiquitous
But unnoticed to all of us
He's a Divine force
Who can but change any course

At times He is a Destroyer
His wrath means something is on fire
He won't let the Evil move freely for long
No Demon would be spared from His rage-strong
He's the most indignant when sth unusual and untoward happens
He won't rest until he punishes the one who deserves
Gives rewards according to the deeds one does
Has anyone got spared from His Hawk eyes?
He would definitely be showing His other side
No mercy for the malefactor
Wrongdoer would be chastised

His Kind side is so appealing
Showers His Mercy on all beings
He loves us all like our parents do
His vast palace like heart has a place for me and you

His ever pervading form keeps us in awe
He's above all beings, he is just Supreme
He's a Helper, Rescuer and a Benevolent
Always believe and have full faith in Him
He's all permeating, eternal and everlasting
He's the creator, worship Him for everything!

Life

Ah, what is life...it's so uncertain

What is to happen next, none can ascertain

The smiling faces might have so many sorrows behind

Many hardships one would have undergone, none can define

Oh, there can be an ocean of sorrow all through

Some could have submerged oneself into

Actuality might be different from the reality

What we think today, tomorrow may not happen

Life's a mirage

What seems is not actually true

The light that seems to be poured over us

This darkness- demon overlaps and envelops us

Sometimes we are stuck in troubling waters

Nothing is left but only shocking waves

We march forward anyhow in that sea of woe

Shows overselves in the happiest form by our fake smile though

Have you ever found a being without grief

All have undergone some sort of pain indeed
We all are the sufferers in the hands of fate
No one is going to be saved at any rate
Mental breakdown could cause anyone go in distress
Weariness and agonies can take away our happiness

When we know joys and sorrows are the part of life
Why do we give up and lose faith
If miseries come, pleasures will surely occur
Afflictions and adversities make us mentally strong
This journey called life has to move on
Thus folks, never ever give up
Share your difficulties with your family and friends.

Seema ✍

Had I known Earlier..

Had I known earlier we won't meet again
I would have hugged you tighter then
Had I realized this before you won't stay longer
I would not have fallen for you ever

Had it dawned on me,love is not a thing to be stayed
I would not have loved
If I had understood that you were not destined for me
I would never have thought about you even once
Had I known love could be so bitter
I would never have tasted it even
Had it known to me..love ever changes
I definitely won't have crossed your way and kept silence
Had I known that you would change your mind and walk away,
I would not have loved you, pray!

Now I have known and understood everything though
It is so hard to be away from you
It is now next to impossible not to love you

It's way too hard to survive without you

Now it's impossible for me not to think about you

It is not in my hand to forget you

Though knowing you aren't mine any longer

I still adore you and will do ever and ever

Coz love is not a thing to be forgotten

Love is rather a feeling to be stayed forever

Seema ✍

When You Miss Someone..

I can't reach there to see you, though
Sending the fragrant air to you
When the soft breeze touches you gently
Understand that it's me.. kissing you

I can't travel to see you though
Sending the bouquet to you
When you get a whiff of the incense all around
Understand that it's me smiling at you

I have no means to come there, though
Sending this lovely bird to you
When this birdie pops up it's mouth
Understand that it's me saying"I love you"

I may not come to see you though
Sending you a sweet playing flute
When you happen to hear a soft sound
Understand that it's my heart beating for you

The distance is the barrier I can't travel though
Sending the rain shower to you
When you get totally drenched
Understand that it's me hugging you

I am in no position to visit you though
Sending our old photographs to you
When you open to see the album
Understand that it's me remembering you

We have been away from each other though
Our all old memories are captured in my heart, so
When you feel like shedding a tear or two
Understand that it's me crying for you

When someday you feel like seeing me
You can look at the vast Blue Sky,
The Stars, the Sun and the Moon
Understand that it's me looking at you

We may not meet this time though

I will keep sending you the treasure of love

I have preserved for lifetime

Understand that it's the only gift I have for you

Seema ✍

The Poetry of Earth Ceases Never

Everything around seems to be singing

Some Sweet songs that keep buzzing

Twittering birds, cooing doves

These larks and hummingbirds

O listen, to their orchestral merry tunes

Lovely it sounds when a singer croons

Keeps us alive with their euphonious cadence

Symphony of life brings peace and solace

Kids squealing at their play

Infant's chuckle removes our fatigue away

Delightful lullabies sung by mothers

Make their babies sleep in their arms

Tiny- tots sing merrily their rhymes

Amazing it sounds..hear them sing in their prime

Oh, this sighing of air, rustling of leaves

Falling Water from the streams

Relieves us from every stress or strain

Soothes our nerves, refreshes our brain

Somewhere the lark sings and the cuckoo coos
Their echoes thrill and soothe our tired limbs
Chirping birdies appeal to our weary minds
Uplift our mood with their enchanted tunes
Oh, It's so sweet to listen the chorus at the dawn
These birds enthral the audience who had looked drawn
The rhyme and the rhythm of life ceases never
These tiny creatures hidden somewhere keep chanting ever

Carol sung in the cathedrals pleases the senses
Ringing bells in the temples spread out the melodies
Wherever we go, some kinda sounds are heard on
This Earth is a lovely musical place to dwell on
Here, the poetry of life stops never
Music is life, it's beauty can't be replaced ever
Enjoy the lyrics and melodious tunes
Keep singing ye all, some merry songs

Seema ✍

Decluttering… (musings of my mind)

I wanna scribble my scattered thoughts in short version

I have so much to tell

So many stories to share, but..

Infinite thoughts roaming in my mind

I have been rummaging for long

Which ones to keep and which ones to trash

The upheavals in my mind always clash

Make me confounded, perplexed

I wanna scrutiny some vibrant, cool and fresh thoughts

Would be keeping them forever

Rest of others will be shown the passage to outside door

All expelled clutter will relieve me of this burden,

The heaviness I have been loading within for so long!

I want liberty at my end

No chaos, no confusion and no uncertainty

After clearing all the rubbish

Am sure to have a peace of mind

Then a beautiful creation is assured

I expect this from me

I wish to be the master of my own destiny

Want to write my own success story by creating it

Want to own my decisions

Totally devoid of any anything shady and perfidious

Neat and concrete musing is hoped

From the brush and colourful pens of my creative soul

 The perfect piece', I would call it

That thing would give me solace

A calm and tranquility to my mind

Wholly free of all unwanted and vague things

Just clear and plain thoughts, no abstractions

A splendid shape and form of that creation

Then I would be a content being

No more searching for order and peace outside

As it would be dwelling forever within me

As the part and parcel of my life

Never would again be keeping the chaff

When it would be separated from the grain

How wonderful and delightful the life would be then

I will be conquering my own mind

Lemme declutter you, O my mind!

Seema ✑

A Tryst to Remember!

Oh, What a phenomenal and perfect day it was!
When you and me met
Everything looked so fascinating around
Rich greenery and blossoms were found
When you and me met

With you, the place seemed magical and stupendous
I got bewitched by your presence
My dreams had come true, I felt
Yes, I did realise and enjoy it
When you and me met
It was your company, so pure and divine
Meeting of ours was one of a kind
Oh, that magical touch!
That rendezvous can't be bound in words
When you and me met

Hearts melted, breaths mingled when we caressed
What more one can desire than that much
We were destined to meet for some reason
Each moment seemed like a Spring season
When you and me met

Things were different and fantabulous
Flowers greeted us with their awesomeness
Sky seemed clearer, grass greener
Birds sang sweeter, I looked prettier
When you and me met

That cluster of flowers on the side garden
That vine, that spray of floret.. Oh, so captivating!
You and me sitting along, both enraptured
Reminiscence of togetherness we captured
When you and me met

That remarkable day, that memorable day
Oh, our Springing Emotions!
The memories made an event
I just desired you to   Hold on'
When you and me met

It was ours first meeting though

Will be kept in the hearts life long

Now, yearning to meet again

With a cup of coffee sitting beside the rain

Still I remember and cherish the day.... When you and me
met

Seema ✍

A Covetous Call

Come, be my Light
Remove the Darkness
When it envelops me
And make me enlightened

Come, be my Sunshine
Spread your beams upon me
When I need the warmth of love
Hug me tightly

Come, be my Moon
Give me solace
With your glimmer cool effect
So that I can forget all my gloom

Come, be my Inner Spark
Rejuvenate me
Enthuse me to rework
When I get exhaust within

Come, be my Support
Embrace me in your cozy arms
Make my spirits bloom again
When I stagger hard

Come, be my Hope
Make me alive once again
Enthuse me to revitalize
When my inner spirits dwindle

Come, be my Star
Show me the path
When I deviate
Guide me to reach my destination

Come, be my Soul
And mingle with mine
We will dwell together forever
Then I will have nothing to lose

Come, be my Prayer
And let my only wish to be granted
The Almighty would listen to me
When I pray Him to make you mine

Seema✍

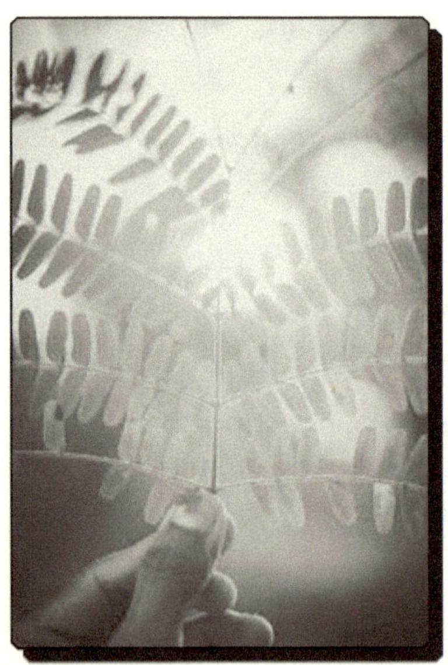

Sun will Rise Again

Glorious and Glimmering,

Marvelous and Shimmering,

O Titanic Star, keep glossing.

What if thy light is a bit pale today, it won't be forever this way!

What if the sky sometimes looks gray!

Never be in despair, come what may!

Let the dust storm pour and rain shower.

Can these forces lessen your power?

You shall always stand tall like a tower.

Hey, Ball of fire' you have a genial grace,

You are the one who always leaves a trace.

Do not worry, show your worth with a bold face.

Never abandon the spark you have within,

This is a tremendous treasure you must retain.

Forget the Inhibition or any restraint.

No one can ever cease your indomitable power,
You are indeed self assured, spread your wings with your warm shower.
Never yield to the odds, neither scowl nor glower.

You shall be known for your invincible nature,
Prove your worth to the world with your unique features.
No one can stand before you, be it any creature.

Come forward, show your brightness to the world around,
Awaiting you to rise, awake and replace the darkness profound!

Seema ✍

Penning You Down

Let me dive in the ocean of your eyes, deep.
I wish to listen to what they speak.
Let me gaze at the immaculate lips of yours;
I wish to find out how they talk without any fuss.

Let me penetrate in your heart within,
I wish to admire that which is pure and so caring.
Let me fondle your soul that dwell in;
I wish to know how it can be so loving.

Let me swim in the crystal clear steam of your mind.
I wish to read how it is so kind.
Let me cognizant of you as a whole;
I wish to compose a poem on you, soulful though small.

Let me comprehend how do you work meticulously.
I wish to learn something from you wishfully.
Let me fathom deep in the bottom of your heart;
I wish to create a beautiful piece of art.

Let me know about you with all my senses.

I wish to master the right words and phrases.

Let me scribble few verses about your life;

I wish to create a masterpiece without strife.

Seema ✍

Stay Humble!

All these trophies, glories and triumphs,
Would one day vanish in some trance.
Your kind disposition will surely remain forever,
Until the end of the world, however.

All these victories and conquests, O man!
Won't be living always, will soon go wan.
The demeanor you display, will have its long lasting impact,
It will get imprinted in the persons' heart.

You may have transcended all blocks,
Entered a Brave New World, no doubts.
Your countenance, however, matters more, for sure.
The humbleness and decency will pay you even more.

Never let the virtues you possess, go in vain.
Let the chaff fly away, just keep the grain.
Stay humble anyway and maintain the poise,
Forget the vices, embrace the kindful essence.

Be you and only you no matter with certain flaws,

None can ever be perfect, but try to be true, nevertheless.

The roadblocks may hinder your paths sometimes,

Never you get astray, keep walking with honest trials.

You may have got the impossible achieved,

Your behavior speaks volumes what you have hitherto received.

Value your disposition more than your winning power,

 Humility' you show, will stand like a Mighty Tower.

Seema ✍

He came like an air,

Went back like a rain shower;

Leaving me all cool and drenched all over.

Me, now like a parched land,

Awaiting for his arrival.

Seema ✍

Pristine Beauty

Bliss it feels to see the wondrous sights
It's a delightful treat to my eyes
Feast to all my senses
Makes me weave thousand fancies
I dream of being there amongst pansies
Ohh, it's so heavenly
These steep valleys
Mammoth mountains
Sparkling streams
Breathtaking views
Marvellous rainbow hues
My heart swings with exuberance
Excitement and exhilaration
Behold, nature is so beautiful
It seems like beckoning
Adorned greenery in the surroundings
It feels I have drunk intoxicated wine
Now, i wish to hold time
To enjoy nature at its best
Wanna forget that makes me restless

Nature is so Divine

It's beauty is unparalleled and pristine

Seema ✍

Burning Candles

Today my heart craves flight
I wish to soar in the midst of height
And I desire to move beyond the sky
Unhold me, unbound me, for I wish to fly

Today I would fly on the wings of my own will
Above the clouds, over the stars, near the sun and the hills
I wish to visit the places where bright light shines
I crave for the Moon to kiss my forehead with its beams

Today I wanna bathe in the warm Sunshine, bright
I wish my tired limbs to get relaxed for a while
I have the heart for getting the smooth touch of happy vibes
I want to be amongst the galaxy in the skies

I would be happy to shake a leg a little
Also to sing on my favorite number with full mirth
Wanna Kindle hopes to get enlightened
My spirits are catching fire, I wanna burn brighter.

Today I have grown one year older
I find myself more stronger and bolder
I am in my high spirits today
I wish to do the most of this Wednesday!

Let me say I am fully blessed and blissed
All through my journey I have had no regrets or stress
Encountered so many lovely people out here in my life
Coz of ye all I keep going and thrive.

With this happiness all around
I wanna play on my new guitar with lovely sound
When the heart sings on merry tunes
All my wishes seem to be fulfilled with a great cocoon.

Seema ✍

Love Forevermore

I am gonna love you forever

I am gonna love you forever

Hey, we may not meet always, however

Distant you may be from me, however

You too have the same feelings for me, I know

You do not show, hide it from me, I know

What love has to do with the distance or showing

It's a matter of heart, not of feigning

We are connected by soul and heart

Will be together, will never be part

For Love is a feeling that remains in the heart

It's a passion for the lovers to play their part

Sweet is this thing if it remains till last

None of the two ever goes apart

Loving someone is a kinda pleasure

A divine bliss it provides which is a treasure

Mine is a true and sacred type of love for you

It will be the same until my last, very true

My love for you will remain ineffable

Will go on increasing with time, always celestial

I would like to write your name in the stars above

Will never be erased, but true and very pure

I am always gonna love you

I am always gonna love you

Seema ✍

When Silence Speaks...

The silence in you does speak
It rather speaks volumes
When your lips are sealed
Your eyes, alluring and tempting eyes, speak
They speak what I wanna hear

When your eyes meet mine, lure me
Entice me, tempt me promptly
That gesture, oh..so very captivating!
Tell me about the matter of your heart
Makes me spellbound

That magic, that charm
When your looks have upon me
Keeps lingering within the whole day around
Makes me intoxicated and totally bound

You are charismatic

Your silent language signals

Your inside perception

What you think

What you feel

There's a wavelength of understanding

That flows through you

Towards me

Saying a lot

Expressing everything

Making me alive again

Seema ✍

The Best Part Of Me is You

All my desires, my longings and my yearnings
Meet only in you
I get that all
What my heart wishes for
My heart is your abode
A safe chamber
Like my heart beat
You dwell there

The sonorous sound that I hear
Resonates within all over
The music you play on my heart s keypad
Keeps me delighted and jovial
Melody of my life keeps buzzing
You are the reason to keep me in elation
These never ending heart beats
Keep flowing and let me keep going

You are so much intertwined into me
Like an air
I breathe you
You are a part of me
My heart throb
Your pulsating sound
Pours out sweet melody
In my ears

You, my life-source,
Very precious indeed
And, the best part of me is you
I am alive till you keep playing
Soothing tunes, chanting musical notes
Keep reverberating
Let's give forth to emotional tunes
They will keep echoing life-long

Seema ✍

Persona With an Unbeatable Spirit!

She kept on walking

Though the road was long and pebbly

And bushes laid on the path

None could but stop her..

Her indomitable will made her go along

Without stop

Without pause

Though her feet profusely bled

She got drenched in sweat

She was just chasing

Her dreams

Her aspirations

She had a will of iron

That kept her going

There was a war

Between her invincible power

And the temptations around her

She chose her burning spirit and zeal

Over the greeds and lures
She had no regrets
With her choice
She kept on treading
Marched ahead
Of the hindrances
Paving way to her success
Carried on
With kindling heart
In high spirits
Went on scaling heights
Never did she turn back
Just over and above
Upper and higher
On the top now
On the topmost level now!

And....

And she won.. !!
It was her triumph!!!
Her triumph over fear!
Success was hers!!!!
She was acclaimed, applauded, Appreciated and admired
Crowned and honored
Given due regard

Got self confidence
Boosted up the morale
Inspiration for all her buddies
All her knowns, unknowns

She was crowned
She had a treasure within

(She is none other than every woman's inner self)

Seema ✍

(This write up is for the women folks who give up in the mid way succumbing to many odds they encounter in their lives. But in every woman's heart, there is a spirit to move ahead. The only need is to be focused and do perseverance to get to the desired goal in their lives)

An Affectionate Bond

Indescribable, impeccable and Unblemished,

Adorned with adjectives even can not be defined;

The bond between a mother and a daughter can not be confined in words ever;

This kind of kinship is never to be found elsewhere.

Sweetest is the feeling you can't sum up in a verse or two,

Writing an epic even would not be suffice to do.

Beauty that lies in this bond is, no doubt, adorable;

Unique is the bond that is very special and unimaginable.

The mutual understanding between the two lasts for ages,

The worth of this bond can't be bound in a few pages.

A mother understands her baby's language even from her womb;

With growing in years, the bond becomes more intense and strong.

Affection, adoration and endearment lie between the two,

There's a superb affinity and tender feelings, very true;

Closeness, love and fondness flows freely;

Like true friends, they share all the things merrily.

With age, a daughter becomes her mum's bosom buddy,
She cares and concerns more for her, with dignity.
Hers is an amazing role to play in her mum's life;
Supports and aids her in many works without any strife.

A mother would love her kid unconditionally,
She fondles, hugs and caresses her child gracefully.
Protects her and defends her...Come what may!
Her love is unparalleled and unmatchable that always does stay.

A daughter does never feel odd to share all her secrets with her mom,
Since she gets all the support she seeks in her boredom;
A daughter is a kernel to her mother, no doubt,
The connection between the two remains life long.

Seema ✍

Beauty

What is Beauty?

Beauty is not something that strikes the eyes,
It is something that captures the soul likewise.
It is a thing of the innermost self lying at the core,
It is seen in the heart of a person more.

Beauty comes in a true and pure form,
It is such a virtue, you can't ignore.
Beauty is found in unseen things you do;
In your noble deeds, lovely demeanour.

Beauty is not only to be seen,
It is the thing to be felt within.
Behaving well with others is beauty,
Showing kindness and being virtuous is beauty.

You may not be good looking or charming,
But your nice dealing with others will surely make you others' darling.

The things you do make you beautiful and adored;
Beauty is derived from your nature, your temperament, pure.

Hearty deeds reflect your beautiful self.
Beauty is your substance, your core that is quintessence.
Good looking people may not be beautiful at heart;
But beautiful people are always good and elegant.

Intense beauty implies purity of heart and soul.
This is the indispensable part of one's essence as a whole;
Beauty is vision; captured by soul divine,
Beauty is the soul itself, very sublime.

Seema ✎

Writing : An Artwork

Poetry is but a passion for the ones who know;
This is the subtle way to express their feelings and show.
Penning down the thoughts and emotions in verses,
A kinda solace it provides that makes them immersed in it.

Their fingers bleed when they write,
Emotions pour out to the extreme height,
They give vent to their latent feelings;
Overwhelming emotions submerge and the writers dive.

They dive deep in the ocean full of words and phrases,
Jot them down, bring their best creations out and leave some traces.
Their ink as if catching power;
Runs so smoothly with kindling fire.

With a fervour to put the things down in an expressive manner,
They scribble more and more than earlier,
In their write ups they seem to commune with their innermost selves;

They fabricate their artworks to bring forth masterpieces themselves.

A rare sort of contentment the writers get
When their creations emerge out perfect
The ingenious piece of work speak of their prowess,
The dextrous work sparks fire on the pages.

Seema ✍

When You are With Me..

Life seems to be amazingly beautiful,

When you are around.

Your single glance so serene, sees silently;

As though reading my heart's secret emotions.

An aura of your warm presence,

Transports me into another world.

Where my imaginations have no strings, No one can cease
my flying spirits by any means!

An irresistible desire to have you,

Lies upon my heart,

Urges me to whisper to you;

Constantly, consistently... I just want you.

"Hold on..Just stay a bit more..don't go now",

My heart feels like saying in a silent tone.

Springing emotions when overflow,

Keeps you on hold in persuasion.

And you listen to my secret language, stay,
Making me delightful, brimming with smiles, I sway in elation.
Passionately I gaze at you with rapt attention.
Oh, that charm and that spell..totally Intoxicating!

My heart weaves thousands dreams when I see you,
In my fantasies I reach several miles away;
Where all dreams seem to come true.
Oh, in that fairy land, I wish to lose myself in you.

The moments spent with you, become eternal,
They remain perpetual and forever,
In my mind and soul they reside permanent.
Those times are my priceless treasure.

When you are with me,
Life seems to be a rainbow
You colour my life and paint it anew.
Your essence has so much of me now.

You leave the traces of you in my soul,
When you depart, I do wish again to see you even more.
My all desires start with you and weave new dreams with you.

When you are with me,
I am happier than ever.
When you are with me
I am joyous and merrier.

Seema

Rain

Silvery showers
Falling from heaven
Pearly looks
Oh, such a marvel!

Shimmering drops
Hearts zooming
Ecstatic souls
Feel like dancing!

Oozing downpour
Adorning garden
Like dainty jewelry
Love from skies showering!

Trickling melodies
Lovely outpouring
Awakening souls
Enlightened minds!

Coolness in abundance
Warming hearts
Delightful sights
Umbrellas in myriad hues!

Oh, such soul- stirring weather!
Drizzling and this swish-swoosh
Swinging emotions
It's a pure bliss!

Lush greenery, sublime beauties
Splendid sceneries
Ornate flowers
Provide soothing delights!
These gracious drops
Pulling the heartstrings
Souls in full bloom
Forget all gloom!

Seema ✍

Never, Never, Never Give Up!!

You may not always get what you have desired,
Success might not be at your feet you would have aspired,
You might have been beaten after many trials;
Never give up even when stuck in deep mire.

For failures are the stepping stones to success,
Learn to rise again when you fall in a trash.
Sooner or later you will watch the sunrise,
Every sunset has a promise to let dawn to replace.

Have little more patience, O tired traveller!
Destination is not too far, just walk a bit more.
If winter comes, can spring be far behind?
Thus, keep walking, do not lag behind.

On each step you will encounter burning fires,
Blazes of that have to be extinguished without being tired.
This life is an ordeal you have to pass it anyhow;

All the hardships you come across have to be overcome now.

Fear not, you are near your dream you had seen,
You will soon touch the winning goal and feel amazing.
How the success seems from very close, O man!
You are gonna touch it in a very short while.

Seema ✍

Come Over!

Do not come to me like the fleeting clouds
That are blown by the winds without the rain showers
Come to me like the heavy downpour
That can drench my sore body all over

Or, do come to me like the rising sun, O my love!
Ignite my exhausted spirit and stay the whole day long
And bathe me up with the warmth of thy sparkling beams
Leave the traces of purity of your ravishing rays

O my darling, do come to me like the moon
Enhance the beauty of the darkness like a boon
In the soothing glimmer of thy glance
I wish to soak myself and enjoy trance

O my sweetheart, I don't wish you to come like a wind
That blows away everything when it comes
Do come to me like the air, though unseen but remains there
I would like to breathe you till my last and forever

My love, I wish you to be here with me, forever

Do never leave me but stay ever

I will keep you in my heart like a treasure

Seema ✍

An Ode to Solitude

In my solitude
I have found my own self
That I had lost
Years back
In the humdrum of life
In so much chaos

Now, I have understood
The true meaning of life
The way the life is to be led
And that, Self love is far more important
Than self denial or renunciation

In my solitude I have pondered much:
Life is a roller coaster
An amalgam of joys and sorrows
A journey to enjoy
Instead of finding destination

Solitude has taught me much
I have learnt to accept life
With all its evens and odds or strife
And that, without rain, nothing grows
Learn to embrace the storms of your life

In solitude, it has dawned on me
You shall not get peace by outward shows
And not by being ostentatious or pretentious
But by being simpler, nobler and virtuous
Real contentment lies in doing humble jobs

Solitude is the best teacher
I have tasted the flavor of pains and woes
And have realized
Dainties may have the taste of the tongue
Real taste but lies in chewing bitterness

Solitude has made me feel much more
That life is a slow dance with some trills
Enjoy it's every step and move in
Falling and rising go hand in hand
Scare away your fear into the winds

Solitude has taught me so much
That, how it feels to empathise

Do good to others and make them oblige
Giving is more enjoyable than getting
Kindness is a virtue, go get it as it is divine.

In my solitude I have enjoyed my loneliness
I have chased my passion and have found pure bliss
This piece of writing has been brought forth
With my own thoughts and imagination
Hope, you would enjoy reading it at your rest!

Seema ✍

Know that you are in love

When your eyes sparkle with blithe
There's a genial smile on your lips
Your face radiates and you look gracious
Your let your hair blow like misty waves

Know that you are in love, when
You keep chortling with no reason
You look nowhere more often
As though missing somebody since long

Know that you are in love, when
This universe looks more beautiful than ever
You feel like dancing every time and forever
You swing gleefully like a flower

Know that you are in love, when
Lovely things come your way like a bower
You feel blessed, there's a merriment all over

You want to share your secrets to the world but do never.

Know that you are in love, when
Every single moment you want to know about them
Spend more time with your own thoughts so often
The glimmer in your eyes is brightened

Know that you are in love when
You pace up and down until you get a precious text of them
You deny doing any other errand
Except your main concern, that is them'.

Know that you are in love, when
You drown yourself in their thoughts
You become debonair and laugh lots and lots
Gaily and buoyant, you look vivacious

Your sighing like burning furnace
Is a clear indication where are you placed
In the heart of someone precious
Know that you have fallen in love with someone special.

Seema ✎

Reverie

You are in my thoughts always
As the fragrance with Blossoms
Deep in my core, you stay there
Like my life line

I am always lost in you
Try to find myself, but
I find you
Losing myself is finding you
I have absorbed myself in you so much

In my contemplation I think of you
I write you in my verses
I have scribbled your name
On the pages of my heart
That can never be erased

You are very close to me
You dwell here within me
I have stored you in my heart forever

Distant you may be, however
But not too far or long

I can feel the vibrations
When my heart palpitates
Since you reside here within
Every time, every minute
Like my heart beats

You are at the centre stage of my life
I love you to the moon and back
You reign in my life
You are the kith and kin of my life
Your entity is mine

Oh, my love, in your reverie
I am sitting here to compose
A delightful piece to disclose
The upheavals of my heart
Make me scribble something lovingly
Aaaaaaaaaaa
You are in my musings
It feels great thinking about you
There's something I long from you
I wish to have you forever in my life
Come over, let me whisper in your ears

You are just mine

Seema ✍

Falling in Love

Falling in love does not mean falling literally
Falling in love implies rising spiritually
Rising above the ordinary
Rising emotionally and socially

There comes an upliftment in you, divinely
You feel it when you love truly
Love does a lot of healing
Miseries go vanished and you are left with a beautiful feeling

Love is a spiritual thing
It is felt in the heart, not in the mind
Love raises your power of consideration
It makes you patient and more endurant

Love makes you a pure soul
It brings metamorphosis in you as a whole
Love does not mean falling by any means
It elevates you completely, you no more thrive in anxieties

Love brings an emotional growth in your life
A sweet transformation, which is purely divine
All things look heavenly and delightful
Your mood is uplifted, you remain ecstatic

You get to know what feelings are when you are in love
You become more caring, more sentimental
You understand your partner so well
Love makes you learn to be loyal, a true lover

A person in love abounds in exultation
Love always keeps you in deep exhilaration
All your senses are upgraded with love - vibes
You are tend to get positive energy to imbibe

So, let's fall in love to rise, not to fall:)

Seema ✍

Falling in
LOVE

Visions

Dreamt that I had got my wishes fulfilled
Visioned that I made the things turned bright
Bleak possibilities too turned into reality
All that I had desired, got achieved by me

The dreams were all afresh and anew until the day broke up
Then it dawned on me that they were merely dreams when
I woke up
That I had seen from my eyes in my stupor
Now that I was awake, I was awaken too

Awaken were my senses too
That had been lying listless hitherto
And I decided to show them the light of the day
There I started and decided to set a new mission anyway

Knowing my self's decision, this mind got perplexed
And the heart utterly confounded
How would they be supporting my mission
So, kept staring at me in queer fashion

Pat came the reply from my innermost side,
"Wherefore ye worried", we ll do it, right"
I assured them and set out right away
Away away far from the madding crowd and in some other
way

In deep introspection and still pondering however
I had put forth my heart and soul together
All hand in hand, totally poised
Worked harder than ever, just near the goal post

It was but stormy and dark path ahead, I found
Covered with shrubs, rocks and pebbles around
Heart somewhat got reluctant to move more
My mind kept walking in the windy path till ashore

I, now along with half of my supports remain
Walked some more miles on the rough terrain
A bit I had stepped, there came a shrieky sounds from behind
My heart, in full speed, came running, panting from aside

"Oh, so ready"?, asked my brain in a mocking voice
Hung his neck and downcast, the heart nodded, " I am, it's
my choice".
With new enthusiasm now, me, my mind and heart
Carried on altogether with zeal and zest

We toiled hard, supported each other with no worries
Kept on burning fire when it was cold and chills
Waited for the rain until next dry summers
We kept journeying in all rough weathers

There came us, out of the life's oddities
Got along with each other with perfect poised poses
Now that we had accomplished the mission
A kinda exhilaration and triumph I felt that duration

Seema ✍

Folks, through these lines, I wish to convey a message....if we put our heart, body and mind together, we can achieve the impossible. The only need is to stay focused.

I wrote this poem to motivate my students. Please don't take it as my preaching or speech imposed, I have just tried to write my musings on this positive thing and wanna share with ye all.)

Thanks for reading!

Reminiscences

Ahh, Those portentous moments
Spent with you
Were like ages, imperishable.
Provide me an everlasting joy

Every single moment carried with it
An event to cherish
It was like a Spring that time
When you and I met

That sweet silence
Your amorous gaze
Created an eternal impact
On my soul, I feel it even today

That silent communion
Those springing emotions
Made the sweet love blossomed
It was like heaven, I would say

That Time-Divine was an occasion
We Celebrated, it still lingers within
For it is at my core, deep inside
Gives me never-ending pleasure

Seema ✍

In Memory of My Loving Father

How magnanimous and generous you have been, dear pa!
Your unmatchable disposition kept us all in awe.
You may not be in the physical realms of life now,
We, your kins, still feel your presence in our soul.

When you departed, we were so crestfallen,
The innumerable memories with you, can never be forgotten.
It was unbearable when you left us for heavenly abode;
You will always be remembered for your heart of gold.

Your genial smile and amiable nature,
Your pleasing demeanour would give us so much pleasure.
How adorable you looked when you used to make us laugh!
Your remarkable persona was enough to win anyone's heart.

Your charisma was well known to us,
That wisdom talks used to kindle our hearts.
That appeal in your approach, laced with much humour;
Your all time support, your blessed hand on our shoulder!

The Time-divine spent in your shady grove,
That unfathomable love you showered upon!
Can never be forgotten till our last,
O father, You are fondly remembered, we miss you a lot!

Seema ✍

My World

Wherever I go, I find you
I see my life in you
You always keep me alive
You are my world

I have seen Eternity with you
I wanna live with you till my last
You are my universe
And my heart's delight

We have weaved grand dreams
We will make them true
Together we will create our own cosmos
Where you and me will dwell
Away from this madding crowd

How heavenly does it feel
When we walk together
Hand in hand
With such intensity and soothing delight

It's a pure bliss to have you by my side
O my love, let's keep moving
Till this earth ends
Till our last day arrives

Sometimes you seem to whisper to me
What I desire to listen, just by your eyes
It gives me an immeasurable joy
To see your one glimpse and sight

This world is so charming
That has you in it
Your presence is a boon to me
You are my strength and might

Never you leave me alone, my darling!

I won't be able to survive

Promise to be here with me always

Be it any cheerful day or dark night

Seema ✍

Soul Connection

Distance can not keep the two bodies apart
True love transcends the boundaries all
It's a soul connection,
The matter of the heart

Emotional bond is stronger than the rest
When the two souls mingled together
Though being away from each other,
Create the perfect relation rather

Meeting may not be physical
But spiritual link stays forever
They have a rare kind of affection
Distance can never steal their enthusiasm

The true loving hearts
Know each other's feelings better
Nothing can make them part
Spiritually they live in each other's hearts

Feelings are of foremost importance

Their lives are linked, however being afar

Since they are connected

Heart to heart

Seema ✍

If I Were!!

I wish I were a cloud!
In the midst of the blue, floating around,
I would drop the raindrops on the parch land
Would quench its thirst by pouring, summer bound

I wish I were the moon!
Glimmering in the dark skies
Beams of me would give all guys much solace
Provide them with heaps of happiness and joys
I wish I were the sky!
Would give the folks their mission clue
Dream as big as my vesture blue
And they would make their dreams come true

I wish I were the Sunshine!
Would become the source of laughter and smile
With the rays of my love-light and warm delight
Would illuminate and enlighten million minds

I wish I were a lark!
Singing the melodious tunes from my nest
Unhappy folks would forget their disappointment
Losing themselves in my merry songs and would keep rest

I wish I were an angel!
Who could remove the miseries of the people around
With magical creations of my mind
I just wish my wishes to come true

I wish I were a poetess!
Creating my masterpieces in a row
Bringing forth with something meaningful and true
Giving the world a crisper, sharper and snappier to go through

Seema ✍

Forget me not

When life takes you to the pinnacle of success,
When you get all of your life's best;
When your days are in full bloom and you are in complete rest,
Forget me not.

When you feel you are falling apart,
When there's no one to give you support;
When everything seems to push you to thwart,
Forget me not.

When the rains in your life embellish your garden-green,
When you weave and fulfil your happy dreams;
When You feel you are on cloud nine,
Forget me not.

When life's trudges leave you in deep sorrow,
When there seems none to look for you, morrow;
When you slide in the mire of dark shadows,
Forget me not.

When you hang between despair and hope,
You seem like snared deep in distress with no scope;
When life's journey keeps you in the distant dark spot,
Forget me not.

Tell me when you feel falling deep down inside,
When you feel like crying out loud;
I will share my shoulder to lay on, no doubt
Forget me not.

Seema ✍

Do you remember anything?

Do you remember how much love we were in!

How much intimate we had become!

How we used to share our feelings!

How each day we would celebrate like an event!

Do you remember anything?

How much craving you had for me!

How I longed for your one photograph to see!

Every morning of each day, without a wink!

Every single thing we would share

From your being on diet and then becoming slim, right?

Your losing pounds and eating with dietary choice!

Your feelings on buying a new house!

Do you remember when you showed me your foot's corn injury?

Seeing that I shrieked, you said, " Do not worry ".

Your dentistry treatment and new braces, your singing songs

Just in front of me, since I assured that you sang lovely

Do you remember anything, my dear?
You used to make me feel traveling with you in your car!
Your chatting with me while driving on icy roads,
During chilly winters, then I used to scold!

"Take care of yourself", I used to say
"On that busy road, do not talk while you drive, right away."
Then I would bore you with my nonsense talks on video calls!
Sometimes I won't say a word, but you would understand yourself!

Do you remember anything?
Silence between us too could be expressed
The words I could not say
You were there to listen to me everyday !

Do you remember anything?
Your sending me English songs!
Ed Sheeran and Swift Taylor's numbers!
And my new interest developed in them !

Do you remember anything now?
Do tell me or should I let you know
I still have stored all these memories in my heart

And I keep cherishing them as they are close to my heart.

Seema ✍

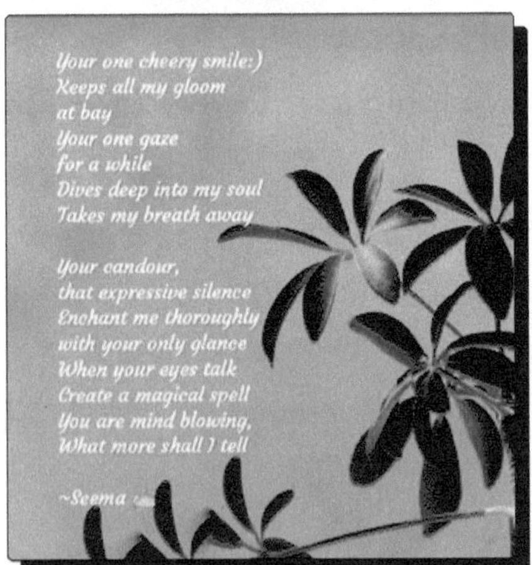

Music

Music is a therapy for the tired minds
It gives you so much solace and peace
Engross yourself in the musical world
Feel ecstasy and forget the rest

Take a break and tune to your favorite number
Be it Ed Sheeran or Taylor Swift
You would like to blow like the breeze
Music is such a lovely thing to make you pleased

Listening to ghazals is awesome indeed
Jagjit Singh ji is the king of this field
Just listen to his soulful rendition
You will have a rare form of passion

Seema ✍

Music

Music is a therapy for the tired
minds
It gives you so much solace
and peace
Engross yourself in the musical
 world
Feel ecstasy
and forget the rest

Take a break and tune to your
favorite number
Be it Ed Sheeran or Taylor Swift
You would like to blow like the
breeze
Music is such a lovely thing to
make you pleased

Listening to ghazals is aweso
me indeed
Jagjit Singh ji is the king of this
 field
Just listen to his soulful
rendition
You will have a rare form of
passion

~Seema

Fallen Leaves

The leaves that are fallen, will take rebirth

They are a signal of hope and coming mirth

This strewn beauty has so much to say

Don't fall into despair, come what may

Let's rake this fall and wait for the Spring to come

New blossoms will bloom and we will again hum

To the sweet music of the swaying trees

When the myriad flora will bloom to give us much peace

Every autumn has a great fall

Looks wondrous when leaves scatter afar

The blowing wind resurrects them and germinates new plants

This is how the different phases play their parts

Remember, folks! Every fall has a rise

Like the fallen leaves if you are in dismay

Keep the hopes alive and spirits high

Very soon you will see the brighter days, pray!

Since, every dusk paves way to dawn

Better days are coming ahead, worry not, man

Seema ✍

Positivity

My heart will keep singing the merry tales
Despite deep inside wrought up in silence
Lies some melancholic traits

Those buried plaintive numbers
Will remain engraved in my head
Until I wish to unearth them myself

I have made positivity my bosom friend
And I have promised it to remain optimistic
I will never ever cheat this mate

Life has taught me the new things to adopt
Hope' is the loveliest thing my heart has got
Never will it be faded, I am sure of it

Life is multi-faceted, I have understood
Sometimes joys, sometimes woes
Everyone makes one's own fate

Why to regret, wherefore complaint
Tranquillity is the key word of life
Contentment too follows afterwards
It's certain

Seema ✍

Let's be the Best Version of ourselves

Let's be a Lantern or a Star in somebody's life

And replace their darkness with much needed light

Let's be a Song in someone's monotonous life

And try removing their dullness with our voice

Let's be the Faith someone can have on us

And let them burst what troubles them outside

Let's be a Stream in someone's dryness of life

And try quenching their thirst with the coolness we can provide

Let's be the Hope in the life of the one

Who has missed even the last rays of the sun

Let's be the Love in someone's life

And sprinkle it's drops to make them drenched and feel relief

Let's be an Apostle of kindness in someone's life

Wipe away their sufferings and woes of all kinds

Let's be the Best Version of ourselves

And do all the good endeavours to make others obliged

Seema ✍

YOU and Me

Your existence in my life
Brings a metamorphosis
In my heart, soul and mind
A rare kinda exuberance I feel time to time

Being with you is a bliss in itself
Those moments are momentous
When we are together
Delighted I become, my mood gets better

You touch me with your pleasurable talks
I am delighted to have you, I am left with no strife
That sweet feeling of your one glance
Inculcates a spirit of love at once

I start weaving various visions
That you and me will be making imperishable
There will be innumerable memories
We will be celebrating them like events

Your occupancy in my heart
Creates an aura of love and warmth
Provides immeasurable pleasure within
Pulling my heartstrings

Seema ✍

Woman of Substance

She dwells with Beauty
She's thronged by it
Outside and inside
She has charming smile, immaculate eyes
Her soul is damn beautiful with rare essence

Her heart is amorous
Dream of million folks
Her entity is heavenly, very celestial
Her companionship soothes the nerves
Tranquilizes the peeled hearts

She is a goddess in the disguise of a damsel
She has an angelic heart
Her demeanor, a class apart
She is an image of Serenity
A symbol of purity

She's Unique, Adorable and Passionate
Her pleasing persona, so affectionate
Impresses upon the core of the heart
She is a Joy for all
Love resides in her soul

Her enamored self appeals the eyes
She is a belle âme, a beautiful soul
Her amatory looks steal the hearts
She is an amazing and alluring lass
She is the quintessence in whatever she does!

Seema ✍

My Soul Companion

Indescribable in words
I am short of this verse
What should I write for you
When you are a poem, yourself

Such magnificent persona you are
In front of you, everything seems small
I love to live forever with you
You dwell in my soul, O, it's true!

I thank the Heavens, and my stars
For, with you, my life blooms like flowers
Your existence means a lot to me
I feel more than glad and glee

Writing few lines on you would not suffice
You are an epic for me, on you I can thrive
You love me lavishly, I owe to you
I too love you dearly, O darling, it's true!

My life begins and ends with you, O my significant other
You are my universe and my world
It's you who complete me, you are my fate
I shower praise on you, O my soul mate

You deserve the best in your life
You have though undergone a lot of strife
I wish for your good and sound health
You are my richness, my wealth

Today is so beautiful, I feel like singing a song
For it was the day you were born on
May God bless you with abundance!
And you abound in immeasurable happiness!

Seema ✍

You are the One...

You are the one who infused
An aura of love and warmth
Inside me
Now my heart is your abode
Live here permanently
Keep loving me constantly

You are the one who brought
Joy and Sunshine in my life
Now, let's enjoy together
The life's wondrous moments
And cherish them forever

You are the one who shared
My past grey days
And laid your shoulders
To let me cry on
I can spend infinite such moments with you
whenever I wish to

You are the one who listened to my silly talks patiently

When everyone left me alone

I felt so morose

But your constant care for me

Made me feel so much cocooned and relaxed

You are the one who has promised

To stay with me

Till Eternity and beyond

And we will walk together

Across the moon and end

Seema ✍

In Love?

You are found engrossed in writing the most!
What's the matter with thou!
Are you in love,
Or your love is lost?

There's some dismal sheen in thine eyes!
And glitter and glow too reflects on thy face!
Are you in love,
Or your love is lost?

Sometimes thy glance has melancholic strain!
Sometimes thou look pale and full of pain!
Are you in love,
Or your love is lost?

Many times, I have read your happy tales.
More often thou are seen writing some sad accounts!
Are you in love,
Or your love is lost?

That time you talked of your millions of sentiments!

Some days after you didn't vent out your hidden emotions!

Are you in love,

Or your love is lost?

Seema ✍

An Ode to Poesy

My Muse! Thou art humbly called to sprinkle thy grace

My thoughts find solace in thy embrace

Come over, let me deck you with my words and phrase

I wish to put life in my musings and leave a trace

Thou art my inspiration, I seek your pleasant stay

I beseech you to be here to enthuse my spirits right away

Anxious is my soul, heart is calling thou aloud

Do come and drizzle upon me some wisdom with gentle sound

Here I sit with a welcome note

Having the word-garland' I have weaved to put on you around

The windows of my heart and mind remain open wide

Please show my writings the doorway to people's minds

Am in love with the new words and phrases

Do come at my humble call to rekindle my thoughts

And infuse a sweet taste in my poems and notes

I wish to fill in them the hues of new craze

O Thou, gush a fire with thy generous praise

Seema ✍

You and My Musings

Merely thinking about you
Sends me in a dream land
With plethora of emotions
Swinging in exuberance,
I feel overjoyed and consummated
I feel like writing

I can dive deep
Into the ocean of joys
Emerging out with the new found pearls
In the form of words
That seem suffice
To inspire me instinctively
To write down a fresh piece

My washed neat brain
Now, fully absorbed
With you inside
Pens down with heartfelt feelings
I shape my words
In the form of muse
Which hardly I can avoid

Ahh, how good it feels!
When you are with me
In my innermost self
And motivate me secretly
To write with wider interest
Which I do consistently and reverently

With your accompaniment
I feel solace
Can't be defined in words
So, love-bound I feel
Some more lines I compose
Don't want to get out of it
Until I am done completely

In that dreamy world,

I want to live for eternity

There seems no end

Of my fancies

Where you become my muse

I hold my pen and with my soul

I try writing poetry

Seema ✍

My Solitude

My solitude and you
Are good companions
They embark the journey
Always together
In my loneliness too
Am not lone or tense

Reminiscences of you
In my lonesomeness
Delight my senses
Fill my vacuum
Though it's all silent
I can talk with you in that silence

Seema

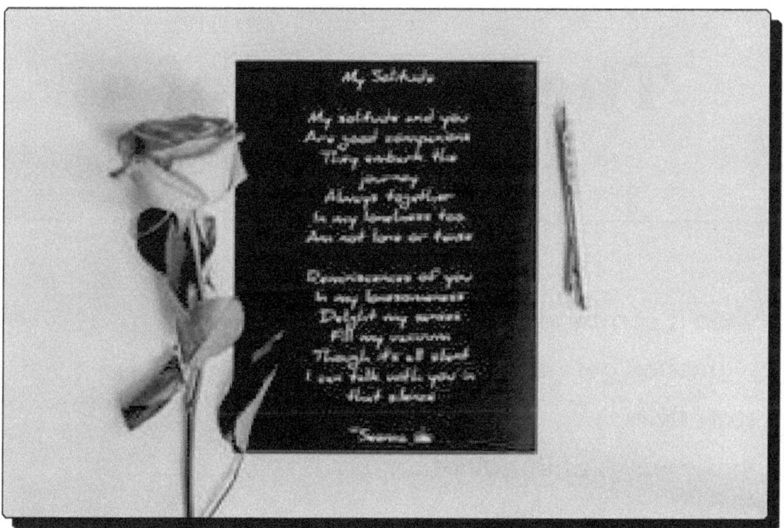
My Solitude

My solitude and you
Are good companions
They embark the
journey
Always together
In my loneliness too
Are not here or there

Reminiscences of you
In my loneliness
Delight my senses
Fill my vacuum
Though it's all silent
I can talk with you in
that silence

— Seema

The Making of a Poem

When it comes to writing
My passion gets mounted
I start flying
On the wings of imagination
And start serenading
Some songs of elation

I start dreaming
About the oceans
Deep blue and it's possessions
Fallen leaves during autumn
About the rainbow
With lovely spectrum
And the lovely lark
Singing across the park

My emotive heart
Flies back to the world around
Beholding gamut of events
And people's participation
The love stories
And the lovers
Sitting beside the forget-me-nots

Thinking about all matters
Give me much inspiration
I start weaving
Myriad of emotions
This way
The making of the poem
Relieves me of all tensions

It gives me solace, it gives me delight
All my senses respond together
In jotting down
The springing emotions
On a piece of paper
Evoking some passion

Enlivened become all my nerves
A rare sort of delight it provides
I take out the words
Lying latent
At my core
In the heart- chamber
And infuse in them some life
With my sheer love and affection

For, poetry is an art filled with emotions
I am in love with it
Call it my craze or passion
It soothes my tired limbs
And gives me so much of exhilaration

I do keep writing
To overcome my glum times
Amidst the ocean of words
I dive in passion
To bring forth
An overflow of emotions
To suit the reader's tastes and likings

I try to compose
A piece worth reading
That could make me content

And I feel enraptured

As I know

A thing of beauty is a joy forever

I wanna remain content with

My work and my small efforts

Seema ✍

Now and Then

Those sweet sacred feelings
That unflinching desires
To be with each other
Some untold stories
Some unknown reasons
To know each other

Then, innumerable meetings
Unfold emotions
Vast and deep like oceans
Unfathomable feelings
Intimate moments when breath mingled
Bliss was that, could be called divine

Deepened love reactions
Oaths taken: For never to get separation
Will be together in all seasons
Experienced a rare kind of exuberance
In our consummation

Then, there came a time
Time became the barrier
Slightly killed our simple pleasure
Ambitions overpowered
Dwarfed became the emotions
Dampened ardours

That warmth, intensity and sensation
That spiritual love intentions
Became secondary
Fervour for finding more material stuffs
Were the foremost things and considered primary

As time would have it
It went on passing
Dug deep the separation
Into the minds of ours
From the earlier intimacy
Linger the past days
Now only in our fancy

We keep wondering
Why all that had happened
When none of us desired
So, let's break the Time-shackles
That came between us

And let's make love more intense
With more ardor and burning desire!

This time, let's cement the ties
Make Love as a prime part of our lives
Never to shun the promises taken
Fasten ourselves with the rope of love forevermore
Dwell in the heart of each other, sacred and pure

Seema ✍

Live your Life Lively!

In the journey of our lives
Sometimes
We do get so much
Exhausted and pressed
All our senses
Seem to have taken rest
Everything looks so gloom
No blossoms even bloom

In the humdrum of life
Engrossed with strife
Seem no pleasures or good vibes
Energy drains out
The glimmer becomes dull
Faint becomes the voice
No charm or enthusiasm is left

In our hearts
Let's cause the spark
Do what pleases you

Listen to the music
That drive you crazy
Go for a long drive
Or sing your favorite tunes

Hang out with ye friends
Shake your legs a bit
Take up the flight
Over the moon
Away, away in the blue
Or sit at the seashore
Breathe the breeze that blows

Awake your senses all
Listen to the lovely call
Someone is there at your door
Welcome to it, be sure
It will be seen stretching its arms
Go, embrace it
You will be returned with your life's charms!

Seema

Happiness is knocking at
your door

The Majestic Beauty: The Moon

How glorious art thou!
Wearing pale yellow attire sitting amidst the blue!
Wherefore art thou hiding so above,
Do you have the fear of getting impure?

You are the one who gleams so calmly
Adorned with the stars shining brightly
Piercing the darkness you emerge out with the mild lights
That gives much solace to the agonized hearts
With thy glimmer, everything looks so embellished
You are a piece of jewel amidst the heavens
Thy crescent shape steals away the hearts of lovers
Broken hearts get relief from their troubles

So, aesthetic and magnanimous is thy appearance!
Seeing you means a treat to the eyes
You have mesmerizing and different shapes
Crescent, round, half and full are a craze

Lone you are though in the vast sky
Never but thou reveal out your heart's plea
Though surrounded by the twinkling stars
Thou shine brighter far apart

Thy beauty is unparalleled and matchless
You are a source of everyone's bliss
You overcome the blackness from their lives
Replace with your shimmering wondrous lights

Thou, a golden plate of round love
Always you spread happiness throughout
People spend their special days
Under your glimmer, in romantic ways

Divine is your heavenly body

You appear on the top of the sky

Night becomes bright with ya company

We all feel blissed enjoying thy captivating beauty

Seema ✍

God, the Almighty!!

Whenever I have stuck in the mire of darkness
You have shown me the way to extricate myself
You have always illumined my grim path
I have got enlightenment in my mind and heart

You keep lifting me up whenever I need help
You never let me give up
Your constant support has always been with me
You have always listened to my heart's plea

There have come the times
I have not even been in my own self
It were you only who had uplifted my spirits
Made me feel to rise again like a Phoenix

I may have achieved the peaks in the time to come
I may have attained the heights of success
I will still be beseeching for your Grace on my head
Obeisance and deference I will pay you forever

I bow before you, in high esteem, O supreme power!
I have a firm faith in thy Gracious Ways,O my Lord!
Your blessings give me a great solace
Keep bestowing upon me thy Divine Grace

Seema

It Were You...

I felt you in the air today
When I was caressed by
The coolness of the breeze blown
As though saying my name far and long

The rustle of the leaves
Whispered a message of your approach
Infused new joys and pure pleasures
Overjoyed I hugged the boughs

I beheld you in the skies too
That piece of cloud had drawn you
It was gazing at me from far above
I swayed with emotions and exhilaration

Sun too seemed to spread it's laughter down in day time
I was soaked with your warmth and sunshine
Joyous, I cried aloud your name
The sky listened and showered upon its acclaim

In the night when the moon opened its gleaming eyes
The light was neither dim not bright
Passed me the beams just in grand style
I knew it were you who made me smile

While sleeping I saw you peeping from the window pane
It were you, you had come in the form of rain
Excitedly, I picked the rain droplet on the tip of my finger
Put it then on my head as a mark of love and respect

I took a dream when I slept
You were there just pampering my forehead
Overwhelmed, I kissed you and retired to bed
The day was spent lavishly with you when you weren't there
yet

Seema ✍

Breathings

In case, in this life

We have to part ways

Take the rest of my breathings too

For, without you

They will be of no use

Seema ✍

Write!

Words speak better than lips
So, write!
Write more to unfold
Your heart's outpouring
Write more to unravel the way
To people's minds
Writing will give your
Agonised mind a rest
So, write!
Write, giving vent to your latent
Heartfelt desires
Your underlying passions
Will find solace
With expressive emotions
So, write!
Write more to get much relief
Penning down will weigh
Your inner pain down
Write!
Write from your core

From your deep inside
Bleed on the paper
With your ink-divine'
With the scarlet- crimson
Of your genuine blood
Write!
Write to bring peace to the upheavals
Of your mind
Your tired soul
Would get pacified
So, write!
Bleed, bleed, bleed out from your heart's pores
Stop not, do write more
Quench the thirst
Quell the hunger
Of the words dipped in the ink of Crimson red
Write!
Cast fire on the paper
With your hard labour
Amour with your words
Create the bond strong
With your musings
That kinship will bring
An Exuberance to your senses
Enunciate what you keep inside
Unearth the secrets

You have kept underneath
Paving the way to people's minds
Write!

Seema ✍

Highs and Lows!!

There comes a time sometimes
We fall in the mire of deep stress
We feel exceedingly alone
Melancholia gets sunken in
All spirits seem to be dipped low
Life becomes quite dull and bored

Darkness prevails everywhere
No light is caught hold of anywhere
No desires, no ambitions
Nothing and no one pleases
You get lose yourself and all happiness
You don't figure out what to do

O folks, never get stuck in the mire of it
Do not get influenced by the evil-luck
Face the things boldly, come what may
Keep going and be happy, anyway
You are the master of your own destiny
Life's ordeals are to be faced boldly

Put life in the work whatever you do
Spark the fire out that lies within you
Think of the merry times that you had enjoyed
And be happy for what good had happened
Don't regret that it is over, nevertheless

Wait for the Spring to come once again
For seasons go on changing time and again
Better days are surely to come soon
In this prospect, uplift your mood
Make your life happier by your own

Seema ✍

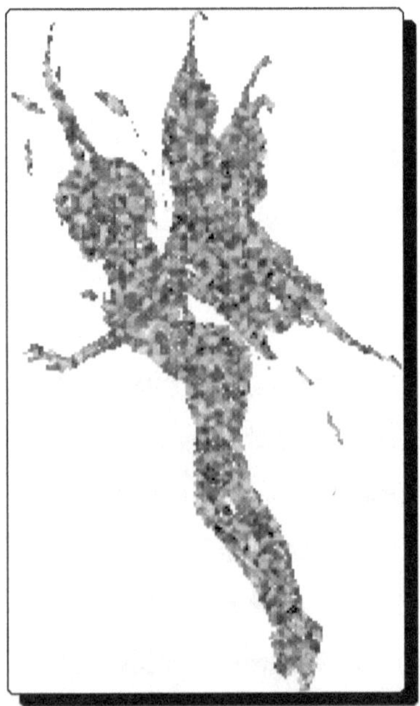

Divine Love

That love is not love
That remains only exterior
Love is the name of a feeling
Which is very pure and spiritual

Heart and soul are the abode of love
You are to dwell there forever
The person you love is your sole pleasure
You wish to keep her like a treasure

As the smile you wear on your lips
Without saying anything it reflects
Love is the thing that radiates on your face throughout
The glow comes naturally when you are in it

The depth of love is felt by the soul
When it is gently touched and reaches the core
True love does not demand any pretentiousness
It can be maintained even with space and distance

Love is felt from the heart and soul

When you are in a mess, it becomes the cure

It does never searches the other's flaws

Rather forgives and always ignores

There may be the love-break

If you are not having any trust

On your mate's talks and interests

Love someone spiritually and do your best

Seema ✍

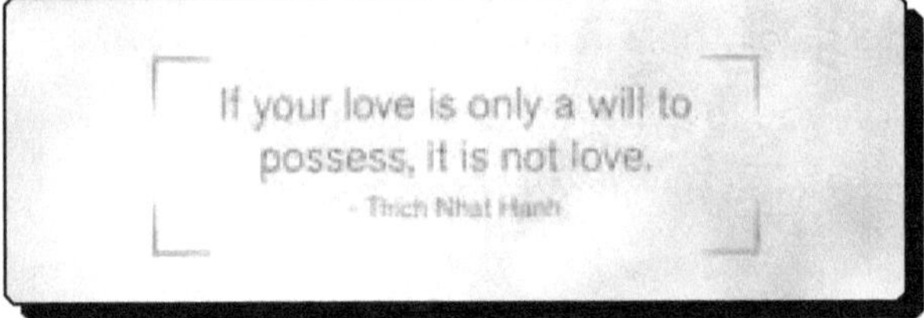

The Outpouring

Inhale love, Exhale poetry
Inhale pain. Exhale the rhymes
The more you love. the more you write
The more you ache, the more you emanate

Your emotions are the tools
They make you create a verse
When you have a agonised or a delightful heart
It too has a role to play a part
To bring forth a poem that says it all

Seema ✍

These things Are Beautiful And More..!!

A divine soul, which is very pure

A laughing face with no malice

The blooming blossoms with myriad shades

A singer with soulful voice when serenades

The ravishing rivulet flowing with grace

The sparkling sun in wintry noon

The glorious moon in summer night

The shining stars that glitter light

The nightingale casting forth it's Melody

A mother singing her kid a soothing lullaby

The face of a soldier on returning home in great bliss

A groom giving his bride a passionate kiss

Bubbles formation when the stone thrown in the deep water

The parents gesture to make their children get married and settled

A teacher's pride when she rewards her student's endeavors
A placid smile of the laborer after a day's work
A happy and contented elderly couple living together

Seema ✍

Deep Love

My love for you is ocean-deep.

Unfathomable indeed

The more I dive deeper

the more I get rejuvenated

In the depth of the love-sea

I feel the endless, everlasting majesty

Sometimes I wanna get drown

In thy troubling waters

And emerged out safer, purer

Resurrecting us both wholly.

Seema ✍